Laz is angry as he runs up
to the punch bag and yells,
"Take that! Take that!"

He has such a lot of anger.

At times he thinks
the stress will kill him.

As he hits the punch bag,
his anger drops a bit.

He thinks back to the bed
with his sick mum in it.

He thinks back to the last hug
and the last kiss.

She was his rock.
She died.
She left him.

When he was a kid,
his dad had left him and his mum.

He had felt angry with his dad,
but his mum was with him to help.

He had felt lost at the time,
but his mum kept him on track.

She was there for him to talk to.

When his mum died,
his best pal, Matt, got him to go
to the boxing club.

It helps a bit with his anger,
but Laz still thinks
he will go mad.

Len runs the club
and he can spot that Laz is sad,
lost and angry.

He asks Laz to have a chat.

Laz stops and sits with Len.
Len asks if he can help.

Laz tells Len that his dad left him
as a kid.

He tells him about his mum
and his anger that she has died
and left him as well.

He sobs and sobs.

"I miss my mum.
She was the best."

Len lets Laz talk and talk.
He tells Laz that it's OK to talk.

"Just get it off your chest, lad.
Just let it rip!"

Laz talks and talks with Len
at the boxing club.

Len sits and lets Laz
get it off his chest.

Laz thinks it is a big help
to talk to Len.

He tells Matt,
"I can tell him stuff.
I can trust him.
It helps to let it out.
I think that I will be OK in time,
with you and Len to help me."

Black Death

by June Lewis

Set 1: Book 1

Black Death
Sound Reads Set 1: Book 1

Written by June Lewis
Illustrations by Amee-Mae Mercer
Edited by Catherine White

Text copyright © Heather Hollands, June Lewis & Linda Richards 2021
Illustrations copyright © Gatehouse Media Limited 2021

First published and distributed in 2021 by Gatehouse Media Limited

ISBN: 978-1-84231-211-7

British Library Cataloguing-in-Publication Data:
A catalogue record for this book is available from the British Library